THE SCAPEGOAT CHILD:

Do Not Embarrass Mom!

BY:

Kemone Hendricks

Written by: *Kemone Hendricks*

Cover Art by: Adriana Poterash

Printing Year, 2025

TABLE OF CONTENTS

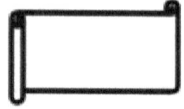

DISCLAIMER

This book is written in a personal capacity. All views, interpretations, and reflections are solely the author's and should not be attributed to any organization, past or present, with which the author has been associated.

*Please be advised that this book is a memoir dealing with severe trauma. **A few chapters, particularly Chapter 1 and Chapter 7, contain descriptions of childhood sexual abuse and physical violence** that may be distressing. Please take care of yourself as you read.*

AUTHOR'S NOTE

The moment you stop normalizing harm and start naming it, is where healing can begin. This book is itself an act of naming, for me.

If you've carried the weight of your bloodline long enough, you're not failing by wanting to redraw the map. You're choosing safety over loyalty when loyalty no longer serves your well-being.

The chapters ahead will blend memory with practical healing: a map of family dynamics, tools for boundary-setting, and pathways to a life that honors truth while protecting the vulnerable parts of you that survived.

You will meet archetypes, learn to observe patterns without judgment, and practice the small, stubborn belief that a life beyond "the only way love is shown here" is possible.

I invite you to also use the workbook I created and start your own act of naming.

ABOUT THE AUTHOR

Servant Leader, Generalist, Critical Thinker and Spiritual Being, Kemone Hendricks is the owner of Evanston Present and Future and Mari Enterprise.

Kemone persevered as a teen parent and multiple abuse survivor. She has and is inspiring countless women; she is a role model to all young mothers struggling to live the life of their dreams. Kemone worked for a multinational firm for 8 years before dedicating her work full time to her businesses.

— INTRODUCTION—

Blood Is Thicker Than Water

"Narcissistic parents use inheritances as a weapon. The cost to be included in their will is your loyalty and being a puppet."

~ Tracy Malone~

"Blood is thicker than water."

We've all heard that. I grew up hearing it, and for most of my life, I just accepted it. It's meant to be about loyalty, isn't it? A promise that family will always be there, that they have your back, no matter what.

It took me a long time to understand that this saying has a darker side.

Blood is thicker, yes. But I've learned that it's thicker because it's closer. Family members are the ones who have the most access to you. They've been there since you were a child. They know your secrets, they know your fears, they know exactly what to say to make you light up... and what to say to make you break. They were there for your traumas. Sometimes, they were the ones who caused them.

When people have that kind of access, that deep, shared history, it's a powerful thing. It can be the foundation for a lifetime of trust and safety.

Or, it can be the perfect tool for control.

I grew up in a system like that. I learned that in my own family, love wasn't a given. It was something you had to work for, something you had to earn, and it could be snatched away in a second. I came to understand that I was living in what experts call a narcissistic family system. That's a complicated-sounding term, but for me, it just meant that one person's needs (my mother's) set the emotional temperature for everyone else. All of us, my sister, my brother, my aunts, we were all just orbiting her, trying to manage her feelings, trying to get her approval, and trying not to be the one who **embarrassed Mom."**

In a system like this, everyone gets assigned a part to play. There's the Golden Child, who can do no wrong. There's the Enabler, who desperately tries to keep the peace and then there's the Scapegoat.

I am the scapegoat child.

If you're not familiar with that term, it's exactly what it sounds like. I was the one who was always to blame. I was "retarded," "clumsy," the one who was "too sensitive." I was the one who was "overreacting." For years, I truly believed something was fundamentally wrong with me. I walked around feeling this deep, heavy shame, convinced that if I just tried harder, if I could just be perfect, maybe then I would be lovable.

I spent so long with those words rattling around in my head that they became a part of me. It was an exhausting way to live, always trying to prove my own value, always feeling like I was failing.

This book is my story but it might be yours, too. It's about how I finally stopped believing the labels that were put on me and started to figure out who I was underneath them. It's about the long, messy, and hard journey of learning to see the system for what it was, not as a reflection of my worth.

I won't lie to you though, this work isn't easy and the change didn't happen overnight. Before you can heal, you have to understand what you're healing from. For me, the wounds weren't from a single event. They were from the environment itself. It was the air I breathed, the rules I learned without ever being taught, and the silence around the things that were too dangerous to name.

It started as a feeling I've had for as long as I can remember. I've lived with a feeling of always feeling unsafe around most of my family members, especially my mom and sister. Even at the times when the words that were coming out of their mouths were kind, or when they had smiles on their faces when looking straight at me, my body would never allow me to feel comfortable in their presence. I didn't know the ways in which they were doing this to affect my energy behind the scenes, but my body was screaming at me, trying to tell me. This is why they say energy never lies.

A knot in my stomach. A quiet, constant sense of confusion, like I was always bracing for something bad to happen.

That feeling takes me all the way back to the beginning, back to Jamaica. I see now that I could never really heal the woman, I am today without first going back to understand that little girl I was. For her, it all started in a dark room, in the middle of the night, with a feeling of chaos I couldn't understand.

CHAPTER 1: BLOOD, BOUNDARIES, AND BEGINNINGS

That feeling of chaos I mentioned, that knot in my stomach... it's not a new feeling that came to me in adulthood. When I really trace it back, it's been there for as long as I can remember. It's not a sharp, specific memory, but more of a thick, heavy fog. A sense of things being unsteady, unsafe, and a dread I could never put my finger on.

That feeling has a home. For me, its address is in Jamaica.

I was born there in 1985. I had an older sister, just a year and a half older than me, so she was my first and closest shadow. My world was her, and she was mine, in the way that only little kids can be. Our family life was... well, it was complicated. That's the word the adults used. I didn't know what it meant, but I knew how it felt. It felt like the quiet, tense air in a room right before a thunderstorm. My father was on the island, and so were other relatives, but we didn't live with him. The "why" of it all was a secret, locked away in the hushed, serious conversations of the grown-ups.

All I knew was the ground under my feet. Then, one day, that ground fell away when my mother made the decision to leave us in Jamaica and go to America. The plan, as I understood it later, was to get established, secure more finances, and eventually file for our green cards so we could all have a better life.

If I remember correctly, I was five years old when she left. At five, you don't understand economics, or green cards, or the kind of desperation that makes a mother leave her children. You only understand absence. You understand that the person who is your entire center of gravity is gone. The world goes from color to gray. The house is too quiet. You wait by the door, listening for footsteps that don't come. You feel a tightness in your chest that you don't have words for, a physical ache that just sits there.

While she was gone, my older sister and I were left with a friend of hers. We lived in that house with her friend and the friend's boyfriend. Even to this day, I still don't fully understand why we weren't left with my father or his family, but this was the arrangement she made. The arrangement that soon turned into a nightmare for both of us.

This is where the fog of dread, that unsteady feeling I've carried my whole life, stopped being a fog and became a sharp, cold, terrifying reality.

That time is hazy, filled with a child's confusion, but there are some things that are sharp as needle in my memory, even to this day. The woman my mother left us with had to work. I remember the house being quiet in the mornings, maybe the sound of a radio playing somewhere, the smell of her getting ready. Then, the sound of the front door clicking shut.

The click of that lock was the loudest sound in the world. It was the sound of safety leaving.

It left us alone in the house with her boyfriend.

He was a shadow in that house. I don't remember him talking much. I just remember him... watching. As a little kid, you don't have the words for it. You don't know what "predator" means. You just know a feeling. My stomach would go cold and tight when he was in the room. I'd try to make myself small, to play quietly in the corner, hoping to just... not be seen.

But he did see us.

He had "games" he wanted to play. That's the word I remember. "Games." The word itself felt wrong coming from him. It wasn't a word that sounded like fun. It sounded like a command. It sounded like something you couldn't say no to.

His games were his way of touching us. This is where my memory starts to feel slippery, like something my brain is still trying to protect me from. He molested us. I remember the feeling of complete, paralyzing confusion. A child's brain just can't hold those two things at once: this is a grown-up, so I have to do what he says... but what he is doing makes my skin crawl. It makes me feel sick and wrong.

You learn to just... freeze. You learn to go somewhere else in your head. You disconnect. You float up to the ceiling and just wait for it to be over.

As awful as that was, there's another memory from that house that feels even heavier, even more confusing. It's the feeling of my sister being gone.

He would just disappear with her. One moment she was there, my shadow, the only other person in the world who understood. The next, he would take her, and they would be gone. The thick, wrong silence of that house would suddenly feel massive. It would swallow me up. I'd be left on the floor, my toys forgotten. My heart would be pounding so hard I could feel it in my ears. Every second felt like an hour. I didn't know where she was. I didn't know what was happening. I just knew, with the certainty only a child can have, that it was bad.

I felt this sharp, hollow ache. I was so scared, and I missed her so much. I didn't know how to protect her. I didn't even know how to protect myself. We were just two little girls, trapped in a grown-up's nightmare, with no one in the world to tell.

That life, that awful, secret-filled normal, just... went on. Days blurred into one another, marked only by the sound of the front door closing in the morning and the knot of fear tightening in my stomach. The dread was constant.

Then, as suddenly as it all began, it ended.

One day, in the middle of the night, my mother was just... there. She had come from America. There had been no warning, no phone call, no "Mom's coming next week." She was just standing in the room, her face tight with an urgency I had never seen before.

I couldn't process it. My brain was still thick with sleep, and the sight of her was so impossible that it felt like a dream. But the way she was moving was not a dream. It was a crisis.

We were pulled out of bed. There was no happy reunion, no hugs, no "I missed you." It was all whispers and frantic, jerking motions. "Get your things." "We have to go." "Now."

I remember a feeling of pure, cold panic. Not just my own, but hers. She was radiating it. Her fear was so big, it filled the whole house. I was terrified, but I didn't even know what I was afraid of. Was it him? Was it something else? I just knew her fear, and it became my own.

We were snatched out of that house and into the dark, cool night. I don't remember packing. I don't remember the car ride. My next clear memory is being on a plane. The cabin lights were too bright. We were surrounded by strangers, and I just remember feeling tiny and completely lost.

We finally landed in America and the air smelled like rain and steel. We were in a new country, a new world, and I had no idea why. The chaos of the flight was over, but the emotional chaos was just beginning.

Now that I am reflecting back on it, I see that I was taken from one trauma and dropped directly into another. There was no time to understand what had happened in that house. There was no comfort. There was just the chaos of the escape, the frantic, unspoken terror of my mother, and a million questions that I knew, even then, I wasn't allowed to ask. The only thing I knew for sure was that the world was not safe, and that everything could be ripped away in an instant.

The disconnect I'd felt from my sister in Jamaica was now a massive, silent gap between us. I kept hearing the adults whispering around me. Soft, sharp sounds I wasn't supposed to understand. Words about my sister, that she "wasn't well."

No one told me what was going on. I was just left with this heavy, aching confusion. I felt this sadness and underneath it all, a crushing, horrible feeling that I had done something wrong, that somehow, all of this was my fault.

Then, my mother came to me.

She found me, and she knelt down. She wasn't the powerful, urgent woman from the middle of the night. She was broken. Her face was puffy, and her voice was thick. She was crying.

Seeing my mother cry like that... it terrified me. It felt like the world was ending.

She looked right at me, her eyes searching mine, and she asked me directly, "Did anything bad happen to you in Jamaica? Did anyone touch you inappropriately?"

Everything in my body went cold. It was like the world stopped.

All I could see was her pain. All I could think about were those whispers about my sister. And in that one, crystal-clear second, I had this overwhelming feeling, this certainty, that whatever had happened to my sister was worse than what had happened to me.

I felt like I was holding a bomb.

I knew, with my whole being, that if I told her the truth, I would be making it worse. I would be adding more pain to a person who already looked like she couldn't take any more. I felt this desperate, crushing need to protect her. To protect my sister.

I looked at my crying mother. And my five-year-old self made a decision.

I lied.

"No," I said.

The change in her was instant. It was like the sun breaking through a storm cloud. The tension just fled her body. "Okay," she said, her voice quick and light. "Okay, okay, good."

She was so, so relieved.

She didn't ask me again. She didn't probe. She didn't look at me a second time and say, "Are you sure?" She just... stopped. She took my "no" like a life raft, and then she stood up, and we just carried on with our day.

I didn't have the words for it then. I wouldn't have them for decades. But in that moment, I learned the single most important rule of my new family. It was a rule that was never spoken, but it was written in stone. It was the rule that would come to define my entire life: **Don't be an embarrassment to Mom.**

Looking back, I see it wasn't even about "embarrassment," not really. It was about her feelings. My pain caused her pain. My truth was a burden. My silence, on the other hand, was a gift. My "no" brought her relief.

This is the moment I see it now. This is where my empathy, my natural ability to feel what other people are feeling so strongly, turned into a weapon against myself. It stopped being a feeling and became my new job. It became my survival strategy.

From that day on, I learned to read the air in every room. I learned to put my own feelings, my own trauma, my own truth, "way in the back." I learned that my job was to manage everyone else's emotions.

This is what it means to be a child in this kind of family system. You don't just get a role; you are trained for it. And I had just passed my first test. I had shown that I was willing to erase myself to keep the peace.

I didn't know it, but I was already learning how to be a people-pleaser, how to make myself small to survive. I had just taken my first step in a dynamic that would rule our lives. I had just learned, in no uncertain terms, who was the center of our new universe. I had just learned that my mother was the queen, and my job, and everyone else's, was to serve the court.

CHAPTER 2: THE QUEEN AND HER COURT

The realization that my mother was the queen wasn't just a childhood metaphor. It was the simple, unvarnished truth of our family structure. It was the law we all lived by.

To understand our family, you have to understand her. My mother was the oldest of seven children. She didn't have much of an education, not even elementary school, because she was put in a position to take care of her younger siblings from a very early age. This story, this history of her sacrifice, was the foundation of her power.

In our family (my aunts, my uncles, my cousins) everyone listened to what she said. She was the final say-so. There was this unspoken belief that everyone owed her. They all looked at her with a mix of pity and respect, as the one who had held them all together and she used that!

She controlled everyone, but not always in a loud, obvious way. She was more like a puppet master, pulling strings behind the scenes. She made sure that no one crossed her. She made sure that no one got "too big." She made sure that, in the end, everything went her way.

I'm using these words ("queen," "control," "puppet master") with years of hindsight. But for a long time, I didn't have a name for this. I just knew how it felt. It felt like her needs were the only ones that mattered.

This is the very definition of what experts call the **Narcissistic Parent.**

It's a person who needs a constant stream of what's called **"narcissistic supply."** That's just a technical term for admiration, attention, and, above all, control. Their entire sense of self is built on getting this supply from the people around them, especially their family. The queen needs her court and the job of the court is to reflect her, to serve her, and to never, ever challenge her.

The mask she wore, the one that showed the world a strong, self-sacrificing matriarch, was airtight. But I saw what was underneath. I saw how she made sure she was the center of everything. To keep that position, her most powerful tactic wasn't to just rule over us as a group. It was to turn us against each other and she was brilliant at it. She knew that if my sister and I were ever truly united, we might find the strength to question her. So, she made sure, from a very early age, that we would always see each other as competition.

I remember she would pull me aside, maybe when we were in the kitchen or just sitting in the car. She'd get this soft, confidential look on her face, like she was about to tell me the world's most important secret. She'd lean in and whisper, "You know you're my favorite child, right?"

Hearing those words... it was like a warm, bright light turning on inside me. It was everything a kid craves. It was approval. It was connection. It was love. I would just soak it in, feeling special, chosen. I'd hold that feeling close, like a little stone in my pocket.

But that warm feeling would curdle a few days later. I'd get into some stupid argument with my sister, and just when I thought I had the upper hand, she'd snap back, *"I don't care, Mom told me I'm her favorite!"*

Just like that, my stomach would drop. The cold, sick feeling of confusion would rush in. We'd stare at each other, both of us suddenly realizing what had happened. The "special" feeling was a lie. It wasn't a gift; it was a tactic.

She didn't even try to hide it. She used to say to us, openly, "I always wanted to have more than one child in case one of them turned against me."

Think about that for a second. She wasn't just joking. She was telling us, to our faces, that her love was conditional. That we were her backup plans. That we were in a constant, desperate tryout for a role that could be taken away at any moment.

This **"divide and rule"** strategy was her main tool for control, and it kept my sister and me locked in a rivalry that would last for decades. We were puppets in her show, and she was pulling our strings to make us dance against each other.

That was her supply.

But a queen can't rule an entire kingdom all by herself. She needs a court. She needs people to protect her, to make excuses for her, and to enforce her will when she's not in the room.

These people are called **Enablers.**

Enablers are the support staff. They are the ones who, whether out of fear, misguided loyalty, or their own pity, protect the narcissistic parent from any consequences. They make the excuses. They look the other way. They are the silent chorus that normalizes the dysfunction, sending a powerful message to the whole family that everything is fine, even when the house is emotionally on fire.

In my family, this was almost everyone else. My aunts, my uncles... they all fell into this role perfectly. They all *knew* what my mother was like. They knew she controlled everyone. They all felt this sense of pity for her, this obligation, because of her story about having to take care of them when she was young.

Because of that, no one *ever* crossed her.

If she did something cruel or manipulative, they would find a way to excuse it. "Oh, you know, that's just how she is." "You know she had a hard life." "She doesn't mean it." Their job was to normalize her behavior, to absorb the tension, and to make sure that the Queen was never, ever held accountable for the pain she caused. They were the ones who helped keep her mask in place.

Enablers are often passive. They keep the system going by not acting, by not speaking up.

But there's another role, a much more active one. There are the people who will do the narcissist's dirty work for them. These are the ones who act as messengers, as spies, and as the emotional enforcement squad.

I call them the **"Flying Monkeys."** The term sounds silly, but the experience is terrifying. These are the family members and friends the narcissist uses to enforce their will. They are the ones sent out to deliver guilt trips, gather information, and put overwhelming pressure on anyone who steps out of line. They become weapons in the narcissist's hands.

I had my most painful and clarifying lesson with this a few years ago, when I finally decided I couldn't take it anymore. I decided to go completely "no contact" with my family.

I knew I couldn't just have a big, dramatic fight. That would just be more supply for them. So, I did it methodically. I started by blocking my family members from all of my social media accounts. Then, I went to our family group text chat (the one where everyone communicated) and I removed myself.

It didn't take long. My mother noticed I had blocked her on Facebook and sent me a text message asking why.

I could feel my heart pounding in my chest, but I knew I couldn't get pulled into an argument. I had to be vague but firm. I texted her back something like, "I've decided to block all family members from my social media and that is my decision and boundary."

It was just a few minutes after our text conversation. Not hours, minutes. My phone exploded.

One after another, texts and calls started coming in, back-to-back from my aunts and cousins.

"Is everything OK?"

"What's wrong?"

"How are you doing?"

Some of them called me over and over.

My stomach twisted. It was a feeling of pure, cold panic. But in that panic, something clicked. I just thought, "That's it right there." This wasn't genuine concern. This was coercion. I knew, in that instant, exactly what had happened. She had received my text, seen my boundary, and immediately contacted my aunts and told them to start reaching out, to pressure me, to get in my mind, and to force me to provide an answer.

It was a tactic. It was how they did it every single time.

This time, I didn't respond to any of them. I just sat there and watched my phone light up, finally seeing the system for exactly what it was.

If you have ever tried to pull away, you probably know this exact feeling. It's the sudden flood of messages. It's the accusations that you are the one being cruel, that you are the one tearing the family apart. It feels like you're being ganged up on, because you are. It's not a coincidence. It's a pressure campaign, designed for one purpose: to make you doubt your own sanity, break down your resolve, and pull you right back into the system.

This is the machine. You have the Queen at the center, the Enablers who normalize her behavior, and the Flying Monkeys who attack anyone who tries to escape. This is the court, the external structure that keeps the family locked in place.

But this external system does something else, too. It creates an internal one. When children grow up in this constant, chaotic battle for love and survival, they are forced into roles of their own. You're not allowed to just be a kid; you have to be a type of kid. In my family, that trauma forged two opposing roles that would define our entire lives: the **"good"** child and the **"bad"** child.

CHAPTER 3: THE SCAPEGOAT AND THE GOLDEN CHILD

When you have two or more children who go through the same significant life event, the same trauma, it affects them differently. That trauma we both endured in Jamaica, and the chaotic, confusing world we were dropped into after, became a dividing line. It sent my sister down one path, and me down another.

I've spent a lot of time trying to understand this. What I've seen, in my own family and in so many others, is that one child will often become an empath, and the other will become a narcissist.

These aren't personalities we're born with. They are survival strategies. They are the masks we create to cope with an unbearable family dynamic. The empathic child, like me, learns to survive by becoming invisible. I got quiet. I learned to be highly attuned to my mother's every mood, sensing her anger or sadness before it even surfaced, and I did everything in my power to manage it. My safety depended on making her feel good.

My sister learned a different way to survive. She adopted a "false self." She learned to avoid being vulnerable, to gain approval by being loud, by being tough, by taking up all the space in the room. She learned to protect herself by making sure everyone else was more afraid of her than she was of them.

After we came to America, that divide between us, which had started as a confusing sadness, became a war. I watched her transform. The trauma that had happened to her seemed to curdle into a hard, sharp rage. She became one of the biggest bullies in school. And she brought that same energy home and aimed it right at me.

She tortured me, in ways that were both big and small. All my friends were scared of her. She seemed to brag about being a bully, to wear it like a badge of honor. I guess, looking back, that tough-girl act was her only protection, her only way to hide the pain she was in.

But when you're a little kid, you don't see that. You just feel the pain.

I remember how much I loved my Barbie dolls. They were my escape. In a house that was so loud and chaotic and scary, my Barbies were my quiet place. I would sit with them for hours, making up stories, talking to them. They were like my best friends. They were the only things in that house that were truly mine.

My sister knew that.

I came into my room one day, and she was there. She had gathered them all up, all of my beloved dolls. And she had cut every single one of their heads off.

I just stood there, my stomach turning to ice. It wasn't just about the dolls. It was the message. It was her way of showing me that she could destroy anything I loved. That she could, and she would, take away any scrap of joy or safety I managed to find. It was a warning.

She would do this, and then she would turn around and call me the most hurtful names, the most hateful words, to get at me. While my sister was taking up all the negative space, I was learning to survive by taking up no space at all. She was loud, so I became quiet. She was defiant, so I became obedient. I was terrified of being an embarrassment to my mother. That fear became my compass.

I learned to walk on eggshells, to read the air in a room, to anticipate what my mother wanted before she did. I became the **"perfect child."** This was not because I was good; it was because I was terrified. I learned to say "sorry" for things that were not my fault. I never, ever spoke back. I poured all my energy into being whatever she wanted me to be.

I found one "safe" way to get attention. My mother loved when her children danced, so I became a dancer. Performing was a way to earn her praise, to get a small piece of the love that felt so conditional. It was my currency. If I could just be the perfect, talented, quiet daughter, maybe I could avoid the chaos.

But in a system like this, even a blessing becomes a weapon.

There was an old saying in Jamaica that if a girl looked like her father, she would be successful and have "good luck." As it happened, I was the spitting image of my father. This became a constant, running conversation within the family.

It sounds like a wonderful thing, does it not? To be the child destined for good luck. Well...It was not.

If anything, I believe it was a curse, a label that painted a giant target on my back.

I could feel my sister's anger every time it was mentioned. It was just one more thing that made me "special" in a way that isolated me. It was one more reason for her to envy me, one more way for my mother to create a divide. It cemented our roles. She was the loud, angry, "bad" one who acted out. I was the quiet, "good" one who was destined for luck.

It took me more than thirty years to understand that those roles were not real. They were not who we were. They were costumes we were forced to wear, day in and day out, until our own skin started to grow into them. "Good child" and "bad child" were just labels, a convenient lie that kept the whole system running.

It took me even longer to find the real names for what was happening to us.

I was the **Scapegoat**. That is the name for the child who is chosen, unconsciously or not, to be the container for all the family's problems. The scapegoat gets blamed for everything. They carry the family's shame, their anger, their secrets. In my case, I was the "good" one, which meant my role was to absorb it all quietly, to be the living proof that the family *could* produce something good, even as I was being emotionally punished.

The question that haunted me for more than thirty years was, *why me?*

I wasn't the loud one. I wasn't the one getting into fights. I spent my whole childhood trying to be perfect, quiet, and small, just to avoid being an embarrassment. So why was I the one who always seemed to be the problem?

It took me a long, long time to understand the most twisted part of this. The truth is, I wasn't chosen for this role because I was weak or bad. I was chosen for my strengths.

A "queen" who rules a family with that much control is also, deep down, the most fragile person in the house. Her entire world is built on a mask, and she is terrified of anyone who might see behind it. The child who becomes the scapegoat is often the one who poses this threat.

Maybe that child is the empath, the one who can just *feel* the tension in the room or sense the difference between a parent's public face and their private one. Maybe that child has a stubborn streak of justice and just can't stop asking, "But why?" or saying, "That doesn't make sense."

Sometimes, it's the child who just has their own light, their own spark of independence. In my family, it was that old saying that I was "destined for good luck" because I looked like my father. That was a spark my mother couldn't control, and my sister envied.

That child is a threat. They are a tiny mirror reflecting a truth the parent can't stand to see.

So, the system has to extinguish that light. It has to break that spirit. The **"scapegoat"** label is the weapon they use to do it. By making you the container for all the family's darkness, they are trying to crush those positive traits. They need to convince you, and everyone else, that you're the one who's "crazy" or "difficult." That way, if you ever try to speak the truth, no one will believe you.

It's the perfect way to silence the only one in the room who might have been strong enough to see.

My sister, with all her anger and lashing out, was what I came to understand as the **Golden Child**. This role is not always about being "perfect" in the way I tried to be. Sometimes, as with my sister, the golden child is the one who gets all the attention, even negative attention. They are the ones who are seen as the extension of the narcissistic parent's ego. My sister's bullying, her power, her defiance... in a twisted way, it was a reflection of the control my mother craved.

As we got older, she also settled perfectly into the role of one of my mother's flying monkeys. By acting as her enforcer (whether by joining in on the name-calling, reporting my behavior back to my mother, or punishing me for stepping out of line), she was doing my mother's dirty work. It was another layer of control that kept me isolated and in fear.

I need to be very clear about this. What was happening between me and my sister was not sibling rivalry. Sibling rivalry is natural. It's two kids fighting over a toy or competing for a parent's time.

This was **Systemic Narcissistic Abuse.**

This was a parent *orchestrating* the competition. She was the one fanning the flames of my sister's envy by constantly talking about my "good luck." Often, she would gossip about us to one another to fuel our separation. She was the one who benefited from keeping us divided.

A parent in a healthy system would be horrified to see one child cutting the heads off another's toys. In my family, it was just the cost of doing business. It kept us from ever trusting each other, from ever sitting down and comparing notes. It kept us from ever looking at her and asking, "Why are you doing this?"

In the end, my sister and I were both victims of this system. We were just two children, wounded by the same trauma, who were forced into opposing corners of a boxing ring we never asked to be in. She was forced to wear the armor of a bully, and I was forced to wear the chains of a people-pleaser.

But those chains were heavy. My role as the Scapegoat was not just about being the "good" one. It was about carrying the weight of everyone else's darkness, and that burden was about to define my entire life.

CHAPTER 4: THE SCAPEGOAT'S BURDEN: CARRYING THE FAMILY'S SHAME

That burden, I learned, has a name. It is the role of the **Scapegoat**.

A narcissistic family system needs a scapegoat to survive. From the outside, the family might look perfect, or at least normal. But inside, it is often full of unspoken shame, dysfunction, and secrets. To keep that illusion of "normal" going, all of that darkness has to be put somewhere. It has to be dumped onto one person.

That person becomes the designated "problem." They are labeled as "too sensitive," "too difficult," or "the weak one." They become the container for all the family's unacknowledged pain. In a twisted way, the scapegoat is essential for the family's stability. By having one "problem child," the system can pretend that everyone else is healthy.

I was that person.

The worst part of being the scapegoat was not just the blame. It was the tightrope.

I lived with a feeling I can only describe as a constant, low-grade hum in my chest. It was the "don't mess up" feeling. I would wake up with it. It was the physical anxiety of knowing my one and only job was to not be an "embarrassment" to my mother.

Don't be too loud. Don't ask for too much. Don't wear the wrong thing. Don't get a bad grade. Don't, don't, don't. I was always trying to be perfect, not because I *was* perfect, but because I was terrified of what would happen if I stopped trying.

But the rules of the tightrope were always changing. It was an impossible, no-win game.

If I failed a test at school, I would feel that awful, sinking shame. I had embarrassed her. But if I got a 100 on a test and my sister failed, I would feel a sharp, cold jab of fear. I was a threat. My success made her look bad, which made my mother angry.

So, I learned to dim my own light. I learned to not talk about a good grade. I learned to feel guilty for any small success, to apologize for it.

This is the impossible dynamic of the scapegoat. Any attempt to defend myself was just seen as more proof that I was "difficult." If I cried, I was "too sensitive." If I tried to explain my side of a story, I was "talking back." If I was happy, I was "showing off."

I was blamed for everything, and at the same time, any attempt to *not* be blamed was seen as an attack.

It is pure, soul-crushing exhaustion. It is the feeling of being "too much" and "not enough," all at the same time. You can't win. You can only try to survive and the only way to survive is to just keep taking it.

That internal pressure, that constant, humming anxiety of carrying everyone else's "stuff," has to go somewhere. It doesn't just stay in your head; it finds a way out through your body.

I went through a period of intense skin picking on my face, especially during the pandemic when the world felt so out of control. It was a compulsive, anxious thing, a physical way to literally *dig out* the discomfort I felt under my own skin.

At one point, my mother had stopped by my house and she saw my face. She just stared at me with this cold, flat look and asked, "What's wrong with your face?"

I remember the instant, hot flush of shame. That old "don't embarrass mom" reflex kicked in. I immediately looked away and lied, telling her, "Nothing, I was just breaking out." I couldn't possibly tell her the truth that I was so anxious, I was tearing myself apart.

But the part that still gets to me is the fact that my mother, the woman who saw my face, said nothing else. She never told me she understood. She never said she had seen it before.

Much later, I worked up the courage to make a YouTube video about that experience, and one of my aunts commented under it. Her words just stopped me cold. She wrote, *"That happens often in our family and no one ever talks about it."*

I stared at that comment for a long time. My breath felt tight in my chest as I read it again and again.

I didn't even know other people in my family had ever been through this. Here I was, feeling like a freak, hiding this shameful secret, and it was a *family pattern*. It was a symptom of our family's sickness. But the rule of silence was so strong that my own mother saw me in the middle of it and still chose to say nothing.

That's the real job of the scapegoat. It's not just taking the blame; it's being forced to carry the family's secrets and symptoms all by yourself, in silence, while everyone else pretends not to see.

To just keep absorbing all the blame, all the anger, and all the things they refuse to see in themselves. This is the most powerful and insidious tactic of all: **Projection**.

I came to understand projection as this: Imagine the narcissistic parent is carrying a heavy, heavy bag. That bag is filled with all their own unwanted, painful feelings—their insecurities, their fears, their shame, their self-hatred. It's too heavy for them to carry. So, they just hand it to you and because you're a child, you take it. You don't know you have a choice.

My mother spent most of her life projecting all of her own negative traits onto me. I can see it so clearly now. When she felt insecure about her own intelligence (she'd had very little education), she would snap at me for making a simple mistake and call me "retarded." When she felt out of control or clumsy, she would call me "clumsy."

The worst was when it came to my future. Every time I told her about a goal, a dream, something I was excited about, she would find a way to crush it. She would convince me that I was not capable of doing it. She told me I was too weak. She made me believe that I just did not have what it took.

It was a slow, steady poisoning. It worked. For the longest, longest time, I really believed something was deeply and fundamentally wrong with me.

This is the most lasting damage of being the scapegoat. It's not just the things they *did* to you; it's the things they *put inside* of you. That critical voice you live with, the one that whispers in your head that you're not good enough, that you're stupid, that you're clumsy, that you'll never be anything.

I want you to really listen to that voice for a second. Does that truly sound like you? Or does it sound like them?

For me, those voices were not just in my head. They were everywhere. They were in the constant name-calling from my sister, and they were in my mother's quiet, crushing words. It was a world of smoke and mirrors.

Chapter 5: A World of Smoke and Mirrors: Gaslighting and Triangulation.

I was losing the ability to tell what was real and what was just their reflection.

That fog, that feeling of constant confusion, was not an accident. It was not just a side effect of the chaos. It was a tool. It was a tactic. There is a name for it: **Gaslighting**.

It is a word that has become common, but the experience is specific and brutal. It is the slow, steady process of convincing someone that their own reality is wrong. It is a quiet, persistent manipulation aimed at making you doubt your memory, your feelings, and, eventually, your own sanity. It is how an abuser makes you feel crazy for noticing the abuse.

For me, this was not a dramatic, once-a-year event. It was a daily poison. My sister, as she got older, made it a kind of sport. She would call me "whore." She would call me "slut." She would call me "stupid." It was constant. Our interactions, every time we were in the same room, it felt like I was just bracing for the next hit. She would say these things and then laugh about it.

The name-calling was the abuse. The **gaslighting** was what happened next.

Every so often, I would get brave. The words would build up in my throat until I could not swallow them anymore, and I would finally say, "Do not speak to me that way." The second I did, it was like I had given them a gift. My sister would laugh in my face. Or, even worse, she would look to my mother, who was often standing right there.

Worst part about all that was my mother, who would join in.

They would tell me I was "overreacting." "Oh, it's just a joke." "You're so sensitive."

In that single moment, the entire script flipped. My pain was not the problem. My *reaction* to the pain was the problem. I was the one who was "too sensitive." I was the one who could not "take a joke." I was the one disrupting the peace by pointing out the wound. She, the abuser, was just "joking." I, the victim, was the problem.

That is a gut-twisting feeling. It is so effective that you start to do the work for them. You start to second-guess yourself before you even speak. You feel the sting of an insult, and your first thought is not, "That was cruel." Your first thought is, "Am I overreacting? Am I really just too sensitive?"

You begin to silence yourself. You learn to just swallow the pain, because you know that speaking up will only bring more ridicule. It is the perfect trap.

That gaslighting fog was incredibly effective at making me silence myself. But it worked even better because it was almost always paired with another tactic.

It was not enough to make me feel crazy; the system also had to make sure I felt completely *alone*. It had to make sure my sister and I would never, ever trust each other.

This tactic is called **Triangulation**, as I mentioned in Chapter 1.

It is a simple, but brutal strategy. The narcissistic parent puts themselves in the middle of two other people (in this case, me and my sister) and controls the entire conversation. They become the single source of information. It is the ultimate way to "Divide and Rule."

My mother was a master at this. We were puppets, and she was pulling our strings. She had made us rivals. It was never about love; it was about control. It guaranteed that my sister and I would always be in competition. It made sure we would never, ever sit down together, compare notes, and realize that we were not the enemy. She was the one manipulating us both.

If you grew up in a house like this, you know that feeling. It is the feeling of never quite knowing where you stand. It is that constant, exhausting competition with your own siblings, a competition you never even signed up for. You feel it in your gut, this sense of rivalry, but you cannot even explain why. It is all designed to keep the children weak, isolated, and fighting for scraps of love, while the parent stays in complete, total control.

These tactics, the **gaslighting** and the **triangulation**, are how they build the fog.

But the fog wasn't just contained within our house. I learned, much later, that my mother and sister were actively working to spread it to the outside world.

It wasn't enough to make *me* doubt my sanity; they needed to make *everyone else* doubt it, too. They were actively doing things behind my back to make our friends and even people in the community see me a certain way.

I found out that they were spreading lies about me, trying to paint me as the "problem child" I had always been labeled at home. The narrative they pushed was as cruel as it was effective: they tried to make it seem like I was mentally unstable.

This is what a **smear campaign** is. It's the ultimate tool of isolation.

Think about how effective that is. It pre-emptively destroys your credibility. If you ever get the courage to speak up about the abuse, who is going to believe you? You're just the "crazy" or "unstable" one. They've already poisoned the well. It makes your friends pull away, confused. It makes the community look at you with pity or suspicion. It leaves you with nowhere to turn, forcing you to go back to the very family system that is destroying you, just to have *any* sense of belonging.

It is the final, brutal layer of the trap. It ensures that even if you find the door, you're too terrified to walk through it, because you believe there's nothing and no one for you on the other side.

The fog itself is not the wound. The fog is just the smoke. The wound is the deep, invisible damage that all this manipulation leaves behind in your body and in your mind.

CHAPTER 6: THE WEIGHT OF UNSPOKEN TRUTHS: C-PTSD AND THE TRAUMA BOND

That world of smoke and mirrors, of gaslighting and triangulation, was my entire reality. When you live in that kind of fog for your whole life, it does more than just confuse you. It fundamentally changes you. It leaves these deep, invisible wounds, not just in your memory, but in your very nervous system.

I later learned there is a name for this: **Complex PTSD**, or C-PTSD.

Most of us have heard of PTSD, which usually comes from a single, terrifying event, like a car crash or a war. But C-PTSD is different. It is the trauma that comes from being in a situation, usually for years, where there is no escape. It is the result of long-term, repeated abuse. It is the trauma of being a prisoner, but the prison is your own home.

For me, the most terrifying symptom of this was my memory. Or rather, the lack of it. I am still recovering memories that were lost to C-PTSD. I have whole sections of my childhood that are just... gone. They are not just hazy; they are black holes. I'll be talking about something, and someone will mention a family trip, or a holiday, or an event, and I will feel this cold drop in my stomach because I have no recollection of it. None.

It is a deeply unnerving feeling. It is like trying to read a book with half the pages ripped out. You know you were there; you know things happened, but you cannot access them. It is just... static.

I learned that this is not a broken memory. It is a survival skill. It is called **Dissociation**.

It is the mind's incredible, built-in escape hatch. When a situation is too terrifying, too painful, too unbearable to be present in, the mind just "checks out." It floats away. You disconnect from your body, from the room, from the reality of what is happening, as a way to protect yourself. You are there, but you are not there.

The problem is, when you "check out" to protect yourself, the part of your brain that makes memories checks out, too. Those blank spots are not a failure. They are not a sign of weakness. They are the footprints of your mind saving your life. It is the most normal response you can have to a completely abnormal, terrifying situation.

But those gaps... they are not the only wound. The trauma does not just affect the past. It affects the present. It affects our ability to leave.

The trauma does not just mess with your memory. It rewires your heart. It changes how you love and who you feel loyal to.

I spent more than thirty years of my life defending my family. I am talking about defending things that are, by any sane measure, indefensible. My sister attacking me with a knife while I was pregnant (I will go into this in detail later). The unbelievable betrayal of her sleeping with the father of my children. These are not small mistakes. These are acts that should shatter a relationship forever.

But they did not.

After the most horrible fights, after betrayals that left me feeling hollowed out, I would still find myself making excuses for them. I would hear the words coming out of my own mouth, talking to a friend who was looking at me like I was crazy. "Oh, but you don't know what she's been through," I'd say. Or, "That's just how my Mom is, she had it hard."

I would defend them to others, and worst of all, I would defend them to myself. I remember this sick, churning feeling in my stomach, this war in my own head. One part of my brain would be screaming, this is insane. This is wrong. Run. But another, louder, older voice would just whisper, But they're your family.

That right there. That is the **Trauma Bond**.

It is one of the most powerful and confusing things a human can experience. It is not love. It is a powerful, chemical, psychological attachment to an abuser. It is a survival instinct that has gone terribly wrong.

In a healthy relationship, love is built on trust and safety. In a home like mine, the "bond" is built on fear and reward. The abuser hurts you, devalues you, pushes you to the brink, and then, just when you are about to shatter, they give you a small act of kindness. A compliment. A "favorite child" whisper. A moment where they are not cruel.

That small crumb of "love" feels like a feast. Your nervous system, starved for any drop of safety, latches onto it. It is a cycle of abuse, and that cycle is incredibly, powerfully addictive. It feels just like love. It is the reason why it is so incredibly difficult to break.

If this sounds familiar, you know this feeling. It is the deep, confusing, sickening shame of loving the very people who hurt you. It is that feeling of knowing you should leave, of knowing this is wrong, but feeling physically unable to, as if your feet are glued to the floor. You feel disgusted with yourself for staying. You feel like a coward.

But this bond is not a choice. It is a cage. It is a trap set by the trauma. It is not a sign that you are weak; it is a sign of what you had to do to survive.

I learned this in the most visceral way, at my own dinner table.

My mother had a rule: we had to finish all of our food. Every single thing on the plate had to be cleaned. I was a child who rarely could finish my food; I just did not have a big appetite. This created a constant, simmering power struggle.

It got worse. Sometimes she would cook things that she knew I hated. It was not because she forgot; it was because she deemed it "healthy" and did not care what I felt. I remember the feeling of dread as I saw her put a plate in front of me that I knew I could not stomach. I was already crippled, I knew I was doomed, because I knew I would be left at that table for hours.

The rest of the family would finish. They would be excused. The kitchen lights were the only lights left on, shining down on me and that plate. Everyone would be in their beds, except me.

I would be left at the dinner table, alone in the dark, with this plate of cold, congealed food. I would sit there for hours and hours. I would cry, silently, until my eyes burned and my face was stiff with dried tears, but no matter what, I could not finish the food. My body would not let me. I was just... stuck. I was paralyzed in that chair. I was trapped in this state of helpless fear.

Sometimes I would be there so long, I would just fall asleep at the table.

That little girl, frozen at the table, crying in the dark, unable to move, unable to save herself... that is the trauma bond. That is C-PTSD. It is not a memory; it is a physical state of being. It is the "freeze" response. I could not fight. I could not run. All I could do was freeze and hope the danger would eventually pass.

I was stuck in that trauma, and I did not know what to do.

You learn to live in that frozen state. You learn to just brace for the impact, to take the pain, because you feel powerless to stop it. You just keep taking it, and taking it... until one day, the abuse escalates. It always escalates.

The cracks in the facade, the ones you have been desperately trying to ignore, suddenly become too big to look away from. The emotional violence you have normalized finally boils over into something so undeniable, so physically terrifying, that it shatters even the "freeze" response. It becomes a matter of survival.

That is what happened to me. The "unspoken wound" of my childhood became a gaping, visible one. The cracks in the family facade did not just spread; the whole wall came crashing down.

Chapter 7: The Cracks in the Facade

Narcissistic abuse does not stay at one level. It almost always gets worse. It escalates. It has to. The narcissist needs more and more control, more and more supply, and they will push things further and further until they are met with real consequences.

For me, the emotional abuse of my childhood boiled over into undeniable, terrifying moments in my teens and early 20s. These are the moments that I spent the next decade and a half trying to make excuses for, to minimize, to absorb into my "trauma bond."

I want to be clear that the stories I'm about to share are just a few instances of what happened; they are not all of the betrayals or acts of violence, but they are the ones that should have been the end. They are the moments that, when I look back, show just how deep the sickness in my family was.

I had spent so long making excuses for it, because they were "family," right?

The betrayal that I think broke something deep inside me was when my sister slept with the father of my children. It's one of those things you just can't wrap your head around. The two people... it just doesn't compute. My brain simply couldn't hold those two facts at the same time. This wasn't a "mistake." This was a cold, calculated destruction. A level of betrayal that shattered my heart to pieces.

Then, the emotional violence became physical.

One day, my sister attacked me with a knife.

I was pregnant.

You'd be amazed at the reason. The reason she came at me, pregnant, with a weapon. It was because I was wearing a piece of her clothing.

I remember that moment in flashes. I could only see cold rage in her eyes. The glint of the metal. My hands, without me even thinking, flying up to cover my stomach. That is **"Narcissistic Rage."**

It is an explosive, uncontrollable anger that bursts out when the person feels challenged, slighted, or loses control. In that moment, I realized this was not just "drama" anymore. This was dangerous.

The violence just kept spreading. I watched my sister beat up my little brother because of some minor disagreement. He was ten years old. She was twenty-one. I saw her corner him. I saw her begin punching him, left and right, punches, punches, punches. I saw tears falling from his eyes as he just stood there and accepted the blows. He did not even try to fight back.

I will never, ever forget the smirk and grin on her face as she did it.

I stood there and watched her do it. I was frozen. I was in fear, because that is what she projected. I was taught to be scared of her.

I even watched her fight my mother. My sister had disobeyed a rule, and my Mom began to discipline her, hitting her with a belt, which was always her punishment. But this time, they were tussling in the kitchen. They had each other by the hair. Then I saw my sister lift up one of the heavy metal stove-top grates. She picked it up and hit my mother in the face with it.

My mother had a huge, open gash on her nose for weeks after that.

The worst part is that nobody talked about it.

Not one word. We all just pretended it did not happen. We were not allowed to talk about what happened. We just went on.

But I could not go on. These were no longer some cracks. This was the foundation itself, proving it was rotten. This was not a family I was **"embarrassing"**; this was a family that was untenable. The "freeze" response, that little girl stuck at the dinner table, finally broke. I realized I was not stuck.

I realized there was no "fixing" this. There was no "helping" them. There was only one path left.

I had to get out.

This realization, was not just a thought. It was a physical survival impulse. The little girl frozen at the dinner table had finally been kicked over.

What I was witnessing was not just a "difficult family" or "drama." I was witnessing the inevitable, final stage of an unchecked abusive system.

This is the concept of **Escalation**. Abuse in these systems rarely gets better on its own. It does not stay at one level. It has to escalate, because the narcissist's need for control is a bottomless pit. They have to keep pushing the boundaries, getting more extreme, to get the same reaction and the same feeling of power. The name-calling I endured as a child had escalated to a knife.

I was also learning about **Betrayal Trauma**. This is a specific and devastating kind of pain. It is the trauma that comes when the very people who are supposed to protect you (your mother, your sister, your partner) are the ones who are harming you.

When my sister slept with the father of my children, it was not just infidelity. It was a complete betrayal that tore apart my reality. The two people... it just did not compute. It short-circuited my brain. The trauma comes from the fact that your protectors have become your attackers, and your brain does not know how to file that. There is no "safe place" to run to, because the danger is the safe place.

I am sharing these stories not for shock value. I am sharing them because I need you to see what this looks like when it is allowed to grow.

This is the inevitable conclusion of a system built on gaslighting, projection, and control.

If you are reading this, and you are in a situation where you are constantly minimizing the **"drama"** in your own family... I want you to give yourself permission to see it for what it is.

If you see your own story in these moments of escalation and rage, please know you are not overreacting. You are not "too sensitive." What you are in is untenable. It is not just "dysfunction"; it is danger.

I finally saw it. I knew there was no **"fixing"** this. There was no **"helping"** them. There was only one path left. I had to get out. That decision was the end of one life, and the terrifying, messy beginning of another.

CHAPTER 8: A PRACTICAL GUIDE TO NO CONTACT

Living through those moments... seeing that look on my sister's face when she hit my brother, feeling the sting of her betrayals, watching her physically attack my own mother... it changed something in me.

The part of me that had spent decades making excuses, the part that would bend and twist and make myself small just to keep the peace, finally... broke.

The lies, the gaslighting, the name-calling—I had learned to live with those. But this was an **escalation** I couldn't ignore. The sickness in my family was not just emotional anymore; it was physical and dangerous.

The decision to finally leave your family isn't a light switch. It's not one, single "a-ha" moment. For me, it was a slow, agonizing dawning. It was the feeling of holding my breath for more than thirty years and realizing, with a sudden jolt, that I was suffocating. My body, my mind, my spirit... they were all screaming at me that I was not going to survive if I stayed.

I knew I had to get out.

But when you finally make that decision, when you finally say to yourself, "I am done," the next question is terrifying: *How?*

How do you actually *do* it? How do you untangle your life from the only people you've ever known, especially when they've proven they'll do anything to keep control?

I've learned that there isn't just one "right" way for this. When you're dealing with a narcissistic family system, you have to choose the path that is safest for *you*. As I see it, there are really three main paths you can take. I have listed them below:

No Contact (NC)

This is the one I ultimately had to choose. It's the complete break. You stop all communication. You block the phone numbers. You block the social media accounts. You don't answer the door. You don't reply to the "flying monkey" text messages. It's not a punishment. It's not an act of hate. It's a wall. It is you, finally, saying, "You no longer have access to me. My life, my peace, and my sanity are no longer available for you to feed on. I am finished being hurt by you." It's the hardest path to choose, but for many of us, it's the only one that allows for real, deep, lasting healing.

Low Contact (LC)

This is a path of boundaries, not a full break. Maybe, for your own reasons, you can't or don't want to cut ties completely. So, you set firm, drastic boundaries. You manage the *terms* of the relationship. You decide you will only see them on a few major holidays, and that's it. You only answer text messages that are about essential family business (like a health emergency), and you ignore all the rest. You don't engage in the old fights. You don't answer the phone "just to talk." You keep them at a safe, managed, emotional distance.

The "Gray Rock" Method

This is a survival tactic for when you *must* be around them. Maybe you're at a family funeral, or you still have to co-parent. The "Gray Rock" method is exactly what it sounds like: you make yourself as boring as a gray rock. A narcissist *needs* a reaction from you—they feed on your anger, your tears, your joy, your explanations. That's their "supply." When you become a gray rock, you give them *nothing*. You give short, uninteresting answers. "How are you?" "Fine." "What have you been up to?" "Not much. Just work." You show no emotion. You don't argue. You don't defend yourself. You just... are. They'll poke and prod, trying to get a reaction, but when they get nothing, they get bored. They'll go look for supply somewhere else. It's a way to be present without being a target.

You see, choosing your path is a deeply personal, painful process. There's no right or wrong answer; there is only *your* answer. There is only the one that keeps you safe and sane.

For me, after seeing that violence and experiencing that level of betrayal, I knew Low Contact wouldn't work. The lines were too blurry, and the system was too sick. I knew "Gray Rock" wasn't enough to protect me.

The only way for me to heal was to get out completely. I had to build a wall. I chose No Contact.

But I knew I couldn't just vanish in a puff of smoke. They would see that as a challenge and the attack would be immediate. I had to be careful. I had to be... methodical.

So, I made my decision. There would be no announcement. No final fight. This was not going to be a negotiation. It was going to be an amputation.

My plan was simple, and it was digital. As I briefly mentioned in chapter 2, I will now share the details I omitted earlier as now seems to be a perfect time to share those.

This was my **Safety Plan**. I was not in immediate physical danger, but I knew I needed to plan for the emotional and digital backlash.

I sat down with my phone. My heart was pounding so hard I could feel it in my jaw.

I opened up my social media. I went to my mother's name. I stared at the "Block" button. My thumb was shaking. I felt this wave of guilt, so thick it was hard to breathe, like I was betraying the first person I ever loved. But underneath the guilt was a tiny, cold spark of relief.

I pressed it.

The world did not end. I let out a breath. Then I did my sister. Click. Then my aunts. My cousins. One by one, I just went down the list. Click. Click. Click.

Then I did the last part. I opened up our family group text chat, the one where all the daily drama and fake "I love you" lived. I looked at the list of names. I pressed "Options" and I pressed "Leave Group."

It was done.

It did not take long. A few minutes later, my phone lit up. A text from my mother.

"Why did you block me?"

My stomach dropped. I felt that old, familiar panic, that instant urge to apologize, to smooth it over, to make her feel okay. I could already feel the guilt coiling in my gut.

But I knew I could not. I knew, from a lifetime of experience, that *any* reason I gave her would just be an invitation for a fight. If I told her the truth, I would be "overreacting." If I told her I was hurt, I was "too sensitive."

This was the moment. This was the first test. I had to **Craft My Message.**

It could not be an explanation. It had to be a statement.

I took a deep breath. My thumbs were cold and stiff as I typed out my reply.

"I've decided to block all family members from my social media and that is my decision and boundary."

I looked at the message. It was the most terrifying, honest, and powerful thing I had ever written.

I hit send.

For a second, there was silence. It was the strangest feeling, like I was standing in the calm eye of a hurricane. I had done the unthinkable. I had said no. I had drawn a line.

Then the hurricane hit and you know the rest of the story.

This was the tactic. This was the bullying. This was the coercion. I was witnessing, in real-time, the system's "all hands-on deck" emergency response. I was seeing the **Flying Monkeys** deployed.

I had triggered what I would later learn is called an **Extinction Burst**.

It is a psychological concept, and it is exactly what it sounds like. When a behavior used to get a reward (the narcissist's manipulation) suddenly stops getting that reward (your compliance), the bad behavior gets *worse* right before it stops. The narcissist makes a last-ditch, frantic effort to regain control. They do not just knock on the door; they start kicking it, screaming, and trying to break it down.

That storm of calls and texts was the sound of them kicking the door. It was a pressure campaign, designed for one purpose: to make me feel so overwhelmed, so guilty, and so *wrong* that I would give in, unblock them, and apologize just to make it stop.

This time, I did not respond to any of them. I just watched my phone light up, finally seeing the machine for exactly what it was.

If you're in this place right now, your finger hovering over that "block" or "leave" button, I just want you to know: your hands are supposed to be shaking. You're supposed to feel sick to your stomach. It feels like the most unnatural, terrifying thing in the world to do. You're pressing a button that goes against every survival instinct you were ever taught.

But that feeling, that fear, is just the training. It's the "good child" in you, the "scapegoat" in you, screaming in panic.

What you are doing is not an act of aggression. It's not an act of hate. It's an act of survival. It's the first and most important step toward building a life where you are safe.

So, take that deep breath. Stick to your plan and prepare yourself for the storm. Because the storm will hit. So how do you prepare for it?

I just walked you through *my* decision. My path was **No Contact**. My plan was digital. But your path and your plan might look very different.

So, let's talk about *your* plan. This is the most important step: **Safety Planning**.

A safety plan is a practical, methodical list of steps you take *before* you draw the line. Its only goal is to protect you. My plan was about emotional and digital safety. Yours might also need to include physical safety, and that is the most important one of all.

If you are in *any* situation where you feel you could be in physical danger, your safety comes before everything else. This is not the time for a "calm text message." This is the time to quietly get your most important documents (your ID, passport, birth certificate, social security card) and any emergency money, and put them in a safe, accessible place. It's about having a "go-bag" packed. It's about knowing exactly where you are going to go (a friend's house, a shelter) *before* you leave. It's about doing it all in secret and getting to safety first. Please, if this is you, reach out to a professional or a domestic violence hotline. They can help you build a plan.

My plan was digital. For me, that meant blocking all social media. For you, it might also mean changing your passwords. Your email, your bank accounts, your phone. It means checking your phone's location-sharing settings. It means doing a digital cleanup so the "flying monkeys" cannot get to you through your friends.

But never ignore the emotional safety. This, for me, was the hardest. Before you hit that button, have your support system on standby. Who is the *one* friend you can call who *is not* part of the family? Who is the person who will listen to you cry and not tell you you're "overreacting"? If you have a therapist, maybe schedule an appointment for the day after.

You are about to go through one of the most stressful, guilt-ridden moments of your life. Please do not try to do it alone.

Once you have your safety plan, you have to decide on your message.

This is what I've learned about **Crafting Your Message**:

Option 1: The Statement (This is what I did). You do not owe anyone an explanation. An explanation is just an invitation for them to argue, gaslight, and pick your reasons apart. You are not writing a legal brief; you are making an announcement. It should be vague, firm, and all about *you*.

- "I am taking a step back from this relationship for my own health."

- "I am not available for these kinds of conversations anymore."

- "I need to take some space for myself. I will not be responding for the foreseeable future."

- "This is my decision."

Notice that none of these say, "Because you did X" or "You're a narcissist." You are not giving them anything to fight with.

Option 2: The Silent Exit. This is also 100% your right. You do not have to send a message at all. You can just... go. You can block them on your phone, on social media, on email, and just disappear. The guilt of doing this can be overwhelming. You will feel "cruel." But I want you to ask yourself: When did *they* ever worry about being cruel to you? You do not owe your abusers a polite exit.

My way was a single, firm text. Then I put the phone down and I had to be ready for what came next. You can take the approach that is most suitable for you.

CHAPTER 9: NAVIGATING THE AFTERMATH

Whichever path you choose, and however you decide to do it, that moment of hitting "send" or "block" is just the beginning.

I had survived the first, violent storm. I had watched my phone rattle itself quiet, and I had not caved. I had not responded to the **Extinction Burst**.

But what happens when that first, loud, angry storm quiets down? What happens when you *do not* respond, and the rattling at the door stops?

This is the part that, for me, was almost harder. The silence that follows is not peace; It is just a pause. The narcissist, realizing that rage and pressure did not work, does not just give up. They change tactics and your own mind, the one that has been trained for decades to "keep the peace," turns against you.

This is the first few weeks, and this is your survival guide.

After the Extinction Burst fails, the next tactic is what survivors call **"Hoovering."** It is named after the vacuum cleaner, because its entire purpose is to suck you back in. The anger and pressure disappear, and a new mask is put on. This mask is designed to target your one remaining vulnerability: your empathy.

I had to prepare myself for this. I knew it was coming. I would sit in my apartment, and every time my phone buzzed from an unknown number, my heart would leap into my throat.

I was waiting for the **Fake Apology** or the **Love-Bombing**. That text from my mother, or even my sister, saying, "I'm so sorry. I know I'm not perfect. I just miss you so much. I'll do better." Or, I would be waiting for the random text from an aunt with an old photo: "Remember this? We had so much fun."

These messages are traps. They are a performance to make you doubt your own decision, to make you think, "Maybe it was not *that* bad." The instruction here is the hardest one: **Do Not Respond.** Not even to say "leave me alone." Any response, even an angry one, is "supply." It teaches them that the tactic worked, that they got a reaction. Silence is the only move that gives you your power back.

But the one I was most afraid of, the one that I rehearsed in my head over and over, was the **Feigned Crisis**. I lived in genuine dread of the text from a cousin: "Your mother is in the hospital." Or, "Your mother is very, very sick. She's asking for you."

My stomach clenches just writing that. You will torture yourself. *What if it's real?* You feel like a monster. This is the tactic. It is a direct attack on your guilt. Here is your instruction, the rule I had to make for myself: **Do Not Trust; Verify (If You Must).** Do *not* reply to the sender (the Flying Monkey). If you feel you must check, you call a *different*, neutral party. Call the hospital's main desk directly. Call a family member you know is *not* part of the inner circle. Ninety-nine percent of the time, it is a lie. It is a test to see if your empathy is still a lever they can pull.

This leads to the long-term problem of the **Flying Monkeys and Enablers**. This is when the *other* family members, the ones who were not in the first angry wave, start *their* pressure campaign. This one is quieter, and feels more confusing. It is the "just checking in" text. It is the "I'm so sad the family is being torn apart" message.

You have to be just as firm with them. This is the **"One-Strike Rule"** I had to learn. For the first "concerned" text from one of these enablers, you give them one clear, firm reply. Something like this: "I appreciate you reaching out, but I am not discussing this. This is a private matter." That's it.

If they respect it, maybe that relationship can be salvaged someday, far in the future. But if they push, even once... if they write back, "But your mother is just so sad..." or "I think you're being too harsh..." then boom.

They have shown their loyalty. They are not a safe person for you. They get blocked, too. No exceptions.

But do remind yourself that the external battle with the hoovering and the flying monkeys is exhausting. You will feel like you are at war, constantly on high alert, checking your phone with a sense of dread.

But the real, agonizing battle is not with them. It is the war inside your own head.

The enemy you cannot block is **Guilt**. The **Obligation**.

This, for me, was the hardest part of all. The "don't embarrass Mom" rule that had been drilled into me since I was five years old did not just disappear because I blocked her number. That training was two decades deep. It was not just a thought; It was a physical part of me, a reflex.

Even with my phone completely silent, I would be sitting on my sofa, and this wave of guilt would just wash over me, so thick it felt like I was drowning. I would wake up at three in the morning, my heart pounding, with this one, crushing, core belief: "I am a bad person."

I am a horrible, cruel daughter. I am tearing the family apart. I am breaking my mother's heart. I could *hear* her voice in my head. I could feel the weight of my aunts' disappointment.

This is the conditioned guilt. It is the abuser's "inside man." It is the programming they installed in you to make sure you would *never* leave. Its only job is to get you to feel so awful that you come crawling back to the system.

I would feel this intense, vibrating, *itchy* feeling all over my skin. It was the physical urge to pick up the phone, call my mother, and apologize... just to make this horrible feeling *stop*. I just wanted relief.

This is the moment you have to fight for your new life. I had to learn to sit with that feeling, and I had to find tools to survive it.

My most important tool was a **reframe**. I had to learn to see that feeling for what it was. I had to teach myself this, over and over: This feeling is not a compass. It is not "truth" telling me I am wrong. This feeling is the *trauma* leaving my body. It is the sound of the old programming breaking. I was not feeling guilty because I *was* bad; I was feeling guilty because I had been *trained* so well.

Once I reframed it, I had to learn to sit with it. I called it **"Surfing the Wave."**

When that wave of guilt would hit, my only job was to *not* act. I would look at the clock. I would tell myself, "I can feel this for fifteen minutes. I will not die from this feeling. It is just a feeling. But if I make that call, I am right back in the cage." I would ride it out. I would get up, make tea, splash cold water on my face, anything to ride that wave until it crested and passed. And it *always* passed.

When the feeling was too strong, I had to have a mantra ready. I had to have a new voice to replace the old ones. I would say it out loud in my empty apartment: "My safety is more important than their feelings." "I am allowed to be safe." "I am not responsible for her happiness." I would just repeat it, over and over. It was my anchor in the storm.

This is what **Standing Firm** really looks like. It is not one big, brave moment. It is not just blocking their numbers. It is this quiet, messy, painful, *internal* work. It is the thousand tiny, hard decisions you have to make, day after day, to not go back.

It is lonely. You will feel like you are doing it all wrong. You will feel like a monster. But this *is* the work. This is you, finally, choosing you. And you keep doing it, day after day, until one day, you wake up and you realize the silence you feel is no longer "empty."

It is peace!

But that peace, that new, quiet space, brings with it a question that is, in its own way, just as terrifying as the storm. With all the noise of their chaos gone, with no fires to put out and no one to manage, for the first time in my life, I had to ask:

Who am I?

CHAPTER 10: RECLAIMING YOUR IDENTITY

That question—"Who am I?"—hit me like a physical force. After the storm of the "no contact" decision passed, I was not met with instant relief. I was met with a deep, profound, *deafening* quiet.

My phone was not ringing with chaos. My heart was not pounding in my chest, waiting for the next attack. And in that silence, I completely fell apart.

I would sit in my apartment, and I could feel this buzzing under my skin, this restless, awful agitation. I did not know what to do. My entire life, my "job" had been to be a **people-pleaser**. I was the one who was always trying to be what everyone else wanted me to be. I had spent decades taking on the emotions of other people very strongly, absorbing their anger, their sadness, their needs, while pushing my own feelings "way in the back."

My whole identity was built on reacting to them. Now, there was no one to react to.

This is the central wound of **codependence**. It is not just about being "needy"; it is about having no self. Your "okay-ness" depends entirely on their "okay-ness." You were a mirror, reflecting whatever they needed to see. When they are gone, you feel like you are gone, too.

If you are in this place, that hollow, disorienting "lost" feeling is not a sign that you have failed. It is a sign that you have succeeded. You have finally cleared out all their junk, and now, for the first time, you have space. Now the next step is to start the following process:

1. Identity Reclamation: Finding Your Footprints

Answering the question, "Who am I when I am not performing to earn love?" felt impossible. I had no idea where to even start.

This is where my journey of **Identity Reclamation** began. I learned it was not like "inventing" a new person. It was more like an archaeological dig, and I had to be incredibly gentle.

A lot of this was connected to my journey of recovering lost memories due to C-PTSD. For so long, my childhood was just a collection of black holes, those blank spaces my mind had created to survive. But in this new quiet, as I began to feel safe, tiny fragments started to return.

And they were not all bad.

It would be something small, a flash of a feeling. The specific, warm-cinnamon smell of a certain aunt's kitchen. A song I used to love before I was told it was "stupid."

I was, for the first time, piecing together my own story. I was finding out who I was, not who they had told me I was.

This is the gentle work. It is not about making big, life-changing decisions. It is about asking small, quiet questions. If you are feeling lost, try this: What is one small thing I liked, or think I might like, that has nothing to do with anyone else? A color. A type of food. A walk in a certain park. You do not have to do any of it. Just notice. You are just re-introducing yourself to yourself.

2. The Practice of Self-Compassion

That dig for my identity was one part of the work. The other, equally vital part, was changing the voice in my head while I was doing it.

For decades, the only voice I had was theirs. It was the "projected" voice, the one that called me "retarded," "clumsy," or "stupid." It was still there. If I dropped a spoon, that voice would instantly hiss, *"You're so clumsy."*

I had to build a new voice. This is the **Practice of Self-Compassion**.

It felt so fake at first. It felt ridiculous. But I would do it. I would drop a spoon, hear that condemning thought, and I would literally pause. I would take a breath. And I would say to myself, sometimes out loud, "It's just a spoon. You are not clumsy. It's okay."

I was, for the first time, learning to treat myself with the kindness and understanding I was denied. I was learning to re-parent myself, to give myself the safety I never had.

This is the final, most important step in healing from Codependence. You have to learn to find that validation *from within*. That new, kind voice *becomes* your validation. It is how you learn to be your own safe place, and it is the single most effective way to quiet the voice of the abuser in your head.

3. Identity and Building Your Inner Compass

This work is not just about finding new things to *do*; it is about finding new ways to *be*.

It is about realizing that you, the Scapegoat, were often the most sensitive, most empathetic, and most insightful person in the room. You were not the problem; you were the canary in the coal mine.

This introspective work (the journaling, the questioning, the self-compassion) is how you develop your inner compass. It tells you what is right for *you*, independent of what anyone else thinks.

This is where the final stage of **Identity Reclamation** settles in. It is no longer terrifying, but empowering. It is recognizing your true self (your values, desires, and voice) and starting to build a life around *that* person.

This is your freedom. You are no longer the empty vessel waiting for love. You are the source. And when you are the source, you can finally begin to build a new life, and new connections, that are based on truth, respect, and mutual love. But to do that, you need the right tools, and you need trusted people to help you hold the space.

CHAPTER 11: THERAPEUTIC PATHWAYS AND SELF-CARE

The process of reclaiming my identity, of finding that quiet voice inside me, was the most important work I've ever done. But for a long time, it was also incredibly lonely. When you try to untangle thirty-plus years of family training all by yourself, you feel... lost. It's not just that it's hard; it's confusing. You don't even know where to start and that creates a new kind of exhaustion.

I had to start on my own. I didn't have a therapist at first. It was just me, reading every book I could find, filling up journals, just trying to sit with my own thoughts and figure out what I actually liked, or what I actually believed, without their critical voices in my head.

A lot of that self-work, the hard questions I had to ask and the exercises I was basically creating for myself just to get by, is what eventually became the workbook that goes with this book. It was my own map out of the fog.

That private, personal work is the foundation. No one can do it for you.

But I also hit a wall. I had to face the truth. I could only get so far by myself. This damage, this pain, it didn't happen to me when I was alone. It happened inside a family, inside relationships. I finally realized that to truly heal and see the things I was still blind to, I needed a safe, outside perspective.

For the longest time, the idea of therapy just felt like failure. It felt like I was finally waving a white flag and admitting that I was the broken one, just like they'd always said. But that wasn't the case at all.

You see, therapy is not failure. It is not admitting you are "the problem." It is the most profound and courageous act of **self-advocacy** you can undertake. It is seeking the specialized tools to dismantle the programming that was put there without your consent. It is the first time in your life you will talk about your family, your pain, and your guilt in a space where the only agenda is your healing.

However, when you finally decide to seek help, the sheer number of therapeutic modalities can be overwhelming. At that time remember that it's not about finding the single best therapy, but the one that aligns with the specific way your trauma shows up. Finding the right fit is a process, not an instant solution. The following are some of the paths that were most helpful on my journey, explained in plain language:

CBT (Cognitive Behavioral Therapy)

What it is: This is the practical work of tackling the **inner critic**. It focuses on the link between your thoughts, feelings, and actions. It is excellent for challenging those automatic, negative statements installed by your abuser.

How it felt to me: CBT gave me a way to fight back against the voice that called me "clumsy" or "stupid." It showed me how to stop the thought spiral. When I messed up, the automatic thought was always I am a failure. CBT helped me pause, recognize that thought as a lie, and replace it with something based on reality: I made a mistake, and I can fix it.

DBT (Dialectical Behavior Therapy)

What it is: This therapy focuses on **intense emotional regulation** and distress tolerance. It gives you concrete skills to manage the huge, overwhelming emotions that come with C-PTSD and trauma.

How it felt to me: This was a lifesaver for the moments when the guilt would hit like a physical wave. It taught me practical, moment-to-moment skills to sit with that intense feeling without acting on it. I learned how to use things like temperature or distraction to ride out an emotional flood without resorting to my old coping patterns, like apologizing or retreating.

EMDR (Eye Movement Desensitization and Reprocessing)

What it is: This modality deals with trauma that is stuck in the body and the nervous system. It uses gentle bilateral stimulation (like following a light or holding vibrating buzzers) to help the brain properly process traumatic memories that were previously frozen.

How it felt to me: My mind had dissociated and repressed so many memories, but my body held the fear. EMDR helped my brain file those painful, frozen memories away so they finally felt like they were in the past, not happening right now. It shifted that constant **hypervigilance** response.

IFS (Internal Family Systems)

What it is: This is a deeply compassionate approach that views the mind as being made up of different "parts." It encourages you to approach the wounded aspects of yourself (like the "people-pleaser" or the "frozen child") not as flaws, but as traumatized parts that all deserve compassion.

How it felt to me: IFS helped me stop fighting myself. Instead of judging the "part" of me that was still a people-pleaser, I learned to ask it, "What are you trying to protect me from?" I realized that part was just trying to keep the little girl safe. This approach brought acceptance and profound inner peace, allowing me to finally integrate the broken pieces of my identity.

You deserve a practitioner who truly sees you and validates your experience. Remember that finding the right person is a process, and you might have to try a few before you find your match. But nonetheless it's a map for the war you are fighting inside your head. It gives you the language and the strategies to dismantle the programming. But the trauma does not just stay in your thoughts; it is stored in your body. If you want to be truly free, you have to involve your physical self in the healing.

Therapy is the deep work, but healing is also built on small, daily acts of care. You cannot heal Complex PTSD just by talking about it. You have to involve your body.

For the longest time, I was so confused by my own reactions. I would just... shut down. I thought it was a character flaw, that I was weak.

The biggest breakthrough for me came when I was reading about trauma responses. I read the word **"freeze,"** and it was like a lightbulb went on. I thought back to that little girl, left at the dinner table for hours, alone in that circle of kitchen light, staring at that plate of cold food. I was so terrified and so stuck. I would cry until I fell asleep in the chair, but I could not make my body move. I was paralyzed.

As soon as I pictured that scene, another memory slid right in on top of it. It was that hazy, slippery, awful feeling from that house in Jamaica. That feeling of my stomach going cold and tight when he was in the room, that "gone" feeling when he would touch us. I wasn't just scared. I was frozen.

That's when I finally understood. The story of me being frozen at the dinner table, and that even earlier, disconnected feeling of being frozen after being molested, wasn't me failing. It wasn't weakness. It was a pattern. It showed me that my nervous system was stuck in **"freeze."**

When you live like that, your body is always braced for the next hit. You are constantly on high alert, hypervigilant, waiting for the next strike. The goal of this phase is to teach your body, right now, that it is finally safe. I have shared some practices below that helped me achieve that:

- **Somatic (Body-Based) Approaches**: These are gentle practices that help release the stored trauma. It is about letting the body complete the cycle of fear that was interrupted when you had to freeze to survive. Things like focused breathing, safe movement, or gentle stretching help release the tension, the fear, and the anger that are trapped in your muscles and tissues.

- **Grounding Techniques**: These are your emergency tools. When you get an emotional flashback (that sudden, terrifying feeling of being back in the trauma) you need to pull yourself back to the present. I learned simple techniques to anchor myself immediately to my safe, adult body, right here, right now. It is a way of reminding your nervous system that the danger is over.

- **Daily Self-Care**: This is not about expensive spa days. This is about building a stable environment. It is about making simple choices that are purely for your own benefit, independent of anyone else's needs. Each of these small, consistent acts (eating regularly, sleeping enough, taking a five-minute break) is a tiny vote of self-trust. It is you telling your inner child, "I have this. You are safe now."

These daily practices are not chores. They are acts of profound self-respect. They are how you build a stable inner environment, independent of the chaos you left behind.

This healer's toolkit is yours. It is a menu of options, not a prescription. You are empowered to explore what feels right for you and to build your own personalized healing strategy.

Using this toolkit is how you slowly, carefully, learn to trust your own instincts again. You learn how to soothe yourself, how to tell what is a healthy emotion, and what is just the trauma acting out. You learn how to be safe, inside your own skin.

Once you are safe inside yourself, you can start the next, biggest step of all: learning to be safe with *other* people. You can start building the healthy, loving connections that every survivor deserves.

CHAPTER 12: LEARNING TO TRUST AGAIN

For years, I carried the blueprint of my family's dysfunction into every relationship I ever had. The patterns I learned at home (like feeling bad about confronting someone who wronged me) did not stay in the house; they traveled with me into school, friendships, and later, intimate partnerships. I learned to use empathy as a survival strategy, always anticipating others' needs and pushing my own to the back.

The first step in building a healthy relationship is understanding why you picked the unhealthy ones in the first place.

The way you related to your mother and sister is the original blueprint for how you relate to *everyone*. This is the language of **Attachment Styles**.

My childhood, full of chaos, neglect, and betrayal, did not give me a secure attachment style. Instead, I learned what it felt like to be **anxious** (constantly worried about being abandoned, over-analyzing every text message, desperate for closeness). Or I became **avoidant** pushing people away before they could hurt me, afraid of true intimacy. This is the natural outcome of trauma.

- **The Problem:** When you have a history of trauma, your nervous system is wired to look for the *familiar*, not the *healthy*. A partner who is slightly chaotic, slightly unavailable, or slightly critical feels "normal" to your body. It is the language of your childhood home.

- **The Solution:** You have to learn to recognize this wiring. The person who feels immediately "exciting" and "intense" might actually be triggering the trauma bond in your body. The person who feels safe, calm, and slightly "boring" might be exactly who you need to build a stable future with.

To build healthy relationships, you have to be able to see the signals clearly.

After a lifetime of gaslighting and projection, your intuition can be completely broken. You are trained to ignore red flags and call them "love." I had to actively teach myself what a healthy person looked like.

Red Flags (Things to Run From):

- **Boundary Testing:** They push against a small "no" or constantly try to check in with you, showing a lack of respect for your space.

- **The Charm Spiral:** They are overwhelmingly charming at first (love-bombing), but quickly start to criticize or isolate you.

- **The Immediate Crisis:** They are always in a crisis, pulling you in to manage their emotions (a classic demand for narcissistic supply).

- **No Accountability:** They never apologize sincerely. They say, "I'm sorry you feel that way," not, "I'm sorry I hurt you."

Green Flags (Things to Move Toward):

- **Respect for Boundaries:** They respect a small "no" the first time you give it. They say, "I understand," and they mean it.

- **Consistency:** Their words match their actions, and they are emotionally stable. Their love is predictable and calm.

- **Repair Attempts:** When you have a conflict, they are willing to admit their fault, apologize clearly, and work with you to repair the issue.

- **Emotional Generosity:** They are genuinely happy for your success and can manage their own difficult emotions without dumping them all on you.

3. Cultivating the "Found Family"

The pain of being discarded by your Family of Origin does not mean you are destined to be alone. You have the profound privilege of choosing your own Found Family.

- **The Power of Choice:** Your Found Family is your support network—the strong, chosen network of friends, mentors, a therapist, or even a support group. These are the people who fill the void left by your biological family.

- **Navigating Vulnerability Safely:** Trauma teaches you to protect yourself by closing off. But vulnerability is essential for intimacy. You must learn to open up, but you must do it with discernment. You do not overshare everything at once. You test the waters. You start with something small and watch the person's reaction. Do they listen? Do they validate? Do they immediately make it about themselves? If they prove they are a Green Flag, you take the next, small step.

- **Your New Legacy:** This Found Family becomes your new blueprint. They show you what love looks like without condition, without shame, and without manipulation. They are the people who cheer for your boundaries and who celebrate your true, authentic self.

This is the hardest and most important challenge after leaving the system. It is about trusting your new, healed intuition, and walking toward the people who reflect the kind of love you deserve.

CHAPTER 13: A LEGACY OF HEALING

All the work we have done (the no contact, the guilt surfing, the self-compassion, the hard work in therapy) it all leads to this single, crucial goal: **breaking the cycle of intergenerational trauma**.

You are no longer the victim. You are the cycle-breaker.

When you are born into a narcissistic system, the trauma is passed down like a family heirloom. It is not just about the stories that are told; but about the behaviors, the unconscious beliefs, and the dysfunctional patterns that are transmitted from one generation to the next. My mother, who had to care for her siblings from a young age and lacked a formal education, was herself operating from a place of deep, unhealed trauma. She did not know how to love without control.

When you leave that system, you are not just saving yourself. You are throwing yourself in front of a destructive force that has been rolling through your bloodline for generations.

I had to ask myself: Do I want my daughter and son to carry the same shame, the same hypervigilance, and the same impossible choice between safety and loyalty that I had?

The answer was a sharp, guttural "No."

You are the one. You are the ancestor who decides, "The buck stops here."

But stopping the cycle requires **Conscious Parenting**. It means showing up for your children as the parent you always wished you had. This is incredibly hard because you are building a structure you have never seen before. You are operating without a blueprint.

My childhood was defined by two things: earning love and avoiding embarrassment. I had to consciously reverse those rules for my own family:

- **Rule Reversal 1: Love Is a Given, Not a Reward.** I made sure my daughter and son knew that my love for them was not conditional on their performance, grades, or quiet compliance. I had to constantly check my own reflexes. When they made a mistake, my first urge, thanks to my programming, was to react with anxiety or fear. I had to pause and consciously offer validation instead.

- **Rule Reversal 2: Feelings Are Safe.** I spent my life putting my emotions last. I had to teach my children the exact opposite. I had to create a space where their anger was allowed, their sadness was seen, and their needs were prioritized. This is the only way to raise emotionally healthy children when you did not have a healthy model yourself.

- **Rule Reversal 3: Not Pitting My Kids Against Each Other.** My mother's most effective weapon was triangulation. She made my sister and me compete for her love. She would pull me aside and tell me I was her "favorite," then turn around and tell my sister the exact same thing. It was a cruel game that locked us in a rivalry for decades and kept us from ever trusting each other.

  I refuse to let that poison into my home. I make it a conscious point to never compare my children to one another, especially not in front of them. I don't play favorites. When they argue, my job isn't to pick a winner; it's to help them see each other's side. I am constantly reminding them that they are a team. That their sibling is their first and closest ally, not their competition. My goal is to build their bond with each other, not to make them fight for my approval.

This work is messy, and you will make mistakes. But the difference is, when you make a mistake, you apologize clearly. You repair the rupture. You do not gaslight your child or pretend it never happened.

The final step in breaking the cycle is redefining what those two loaded words mean.

For decades, my family hammered home the idea that **blood is thicker than water**. They used "blood" to mean obligation, ownership, and an unquestioning acceptance of pain.

But you know the truth now: Family is not just blood. Family is safety.

Your **Found Family** (the friends, the partner, the therapist you chose in Chapter 12) is the real definition of loyalty. Loyalty is choosing the people who are emotionally safe, respectful, and loving. It is choosing the people who celebrate your boundaries, not attack them.

- You are loyal to the truth of your experience.

- You are loyal to your new, authentic self.

- You are loyal to the children you are raising, whether they are your biological children or the inner child you are finally learning to protect.

This journey is your legacy. You moved from being the **Scapegoat** (the container for everyone else's shame) to being the **Pioneer**—the one who carved a new, safer path. You turned your personal pain into a powerful, living message: You can stop the cycle. Your story is not one of victimization; it is one of ultimate, hard-won empowerment.

SURVIVOR VOICES: AN APPENDIX

These stories are composite sketches, drawn from common experiences in narcissistic family systems. They will show you that the roles we've named (the Scapegoat, the Golden Child, the Enabler) are real, and that healing is possible for all of them.

Case A: The Golden Child's Trajectory

My name is not important, but my role was **The Golden Child**.

I was the prize. My parents, particularly my mother, would constantly hold me up as the example of what the family should be. I was the one with the perfect grades, the scholarships, the beautiful wedding, the impressive career. I remember being constantly draped in praise, but that praise felt heavy, like a suffocating silk cloth. It wasn't about *me*; it was about her. My success was just proof of her greatness as a mother.

My sister, the scapegoat, was always there to remind me of the cost. She was the one who could be authentic, who could be messy, who could be angry. I wasn't allowed to have those feelings. I learned early on that any flaw, any mistake, or any genuine need of my own was a threat to my mother's image, and it would be met with cold, immediate withdrawal.

My whole life became a performance. I was trapped by the pressure to perform, to suppress my authentic needs, because I was terrified of losing that "favorite" status.

The breaking point for me came in my late thirties. I achieved a huge professional goal, one that should have made me feel triumphant. Instead, I felt empty. I realized that everything I had worked for was still just for *her* approval. The moment I chose to go to a therapist and admit I was depressed (admit I wasn't perfect) that was my moment of recognition of personal needs. It was terrifying, but I finally realized that the cost of being "golden" was losing myself entirely. Now, my work is learning how to be "good enough" instead of "perfect."

Reflection Prompts:

- What costs did the "good luck" or "perfect child" label carry in your own life?

- How did you use perfection or high achievement to cope with the pressure to be lovable?

Case B: The Scapegoat's Resilience and Boundary Emergence

I was the family's problem. I was the easy answer. If something went wrong (if the mood in the house was tense, or if my narcissistic father was in a bad mood) it was my fault. It was always, instantly, my fault. I was blamed for problems I didn't cause and targeted for the anger my parents couldn't direct at each other.

My childhood felt like living with a constant, long-term blame and isolation. I retreated. I was quiet. They called me "stupid" and "lazy" when I was a child. I internalized those labels. I truly believed I was incapable. Every mistake I made was proof of their claims.

My resilience came from a strange place: not having anything left to lose. Because I was never the Golden Child, I never had to be perfect. My breakthrough happened when I realized I was fighting to earn the love of people who simply weren't capable of giving it. I realized the family system needed me to be the problem for *their* stability.

My boundary journey started small. I learned the Gray Rock method first—just being boring and unresponsive. Then, I learned to say, "That's your opinion," instead of defending myself. The shift came when I began asserting simple boundaries, moving from defensive survival to building a new, healthy support network outside of the family. The quiet work of healing is about unlearning the words they taught you about yourself.

Reflection Prompts:

- List three negative traits your family projected onto you. Now, write the factual counter-statement to each one.

- What does it look like to move from a place of defense to a place of simple assertion in a tough conversation?

Case C: The Enabler's Dilemma

I was the Enabler. That was my role for decades.

It was exhausting. I wasn't the narcissist, but I wasn't the target either. My job, primarily, was to run interference—to clean up the messes, to make excuses for the narcissistic parent's cruelty, and to smooth out the tension so that things didn't completely fall apart. I was always the buffer, the person who sacrificed their own well-being for the *illusion* of peace.

I remember thinking I was being the "good" one, the responsible one. I felt trapped in a deep loyalty conflict. I loved my sister, the scapegoat, and I saw her pain. But I was so afraid of my mother's wrath, and so dependent on her fragile approval, that I never spoke up. I kept telling myself, "It's better to manage her than to cross her." That feeling of owing her for her "sacrifice" blinded me for years.

The burnout was what finally broke me. I was physically sick, mentally exhausted, and I realized I was doing more damage to myself than the narcissist ever could. I had to redefine what "loyalty" meant. It no longer meant loyalty to the system. It meant loyalty to myself. My healing started when I chose self-preservation over keeping the peace. I'm slowly learning how to say, "That's between you two," and step back from the center of the conflict.

Reflection Prompts:

- If you've played the role of Enabler, what excuse did you use most often to rationalize the narcissistic behavior?

- What does it mean to redefine *loyalty* as safety and self-respect, rather than obligation and suffering?